The Man
The Mask
The Myth

Ricky L. Taylor

Contents

Acknowledgements

As expected I have to thank my WHY. And that's none other than my princess, **April Marie Taylor**. God gave me all the motivation I needed on March 29th, 2015. The one person in the world who believes in me more than anyone. This one's for you baby! Daddy loves you!

I have to thank my grandfather **Robert Folks** who, while living, read my first story ever and knew it was about me when no one else did. Who, after death, has been my guiding light to greatness. Our time together was short but your impact on me will reverberate through my legacy and with so, generations of people.

To my mother **Cheryl Taylor**: I used to tell people that our relationship was like Michael Weston's and his mom. (Side note *Burn Notice* is a great show). Just like him and his mom, I didn't approve of or understand all of your methods growing up. In the end though I realized that it was all to benefit me and make me a better man. Thanks mom for hardening a fragile boy and forcing him to be a man. The man you always knew he could and would be, even when I doubted it.

To all those I consider family. blood or not, Blood or Crip, Team MAC old friends new enemies, and everything in between, thank you.

I'm sure that you had everything to do with these poems. My art is a reflection of my reality and I wouldn't be able to tell my stories without my co-stars.

I can't leave without saluting my influences. To the poet **Rae Monet** thank you for coaching me through this process. I can always count on you woman. To the poet **Kelli Kocktailz** I owe a good chunk of my poetic career to you. You were my first coach, and you have always pushed me to do more and be better. I wouldn't even be writing a book without you in my ear. Thanks love. Of course I have to thank my brother Mojavi, and everyone else from the ES tribe. I'll get into those details in the next book. I can't forget my man **Christopher KP Ultra Brown**, who also played a role very early in my poetry career. KP gave me my first paid poetry gig in Philly and allowed me to share the stage with Lenora McGee and the legendary Talam Acey. Thank you **Michael Storm Miller** who created a poetic home for all of us in Chester, PA.

Lastly I have to thank one of my idols, the crime novelist, **K'wan Foye.** My favorite author of all time. I once told him that when I was a kid I wanted to be an author. He wrote me back saying "Your a rapper and a poet, and your a storyteller. You already are an author." Words can't describe what that reply did for me.

In closing I will always thank and represent the city that made me **Chester, Pennsylvania**. The city responsible for Jameer Nelson, Tyreek Evans, Rondae Hollis-Jefferson, and now the published author, **Ricky L. Taylor.**

<u>**Introduction**</u>

Wow where do I begin? There are some warnings I will issue. If I had to rate this book it would be PG 14. There is some foul language, provocative and suggestive subject material, and mentions of suicide and self harm. I strongly urge you to heed my warnings some of this CAN AND WILL be **triggering.**

I don't like the idea of restriction or being put into a box so a lot of my work is divided amongst three different personalities. There's Slikk Da Hitman, The MBTM, and the legendary Snack Zaddy, the latter of which we're going to save for the next book. The other two you are about to meet in great detail. Keep an open mind and enjoy! Let us begin!

Part One: Hitman

Slikk Da Hitman

Like all of the men you will meet going forward Slikk is a complicated person but arguably the easiest to describe. His childhood was fun at times but he couldn't help but wonder what life was like outside of his neighborhood. His curiosity forced him to travel and do research about his home. In his findings is where he discovered that he was a part of a marginalized people, whom were systematically oppressed and miseducated.

He was also a victim of this system. Deceived into underestimating the true power deep inside him. One that had been oppressed for generations. He understood that in order for there to be a rebellion, it would require a rebel. Declaring the moniker "Hitman" Slikk has prided himself on precision and impact as it pertains to his work. If nothing this man is accurate, diligent, and dedicated to his cause. The Re-education of his people.

<u>Blinded</u>

I was blinded by the hospital lights on new years eve in 1991 when they pulled me from my mother.
I was blinded by innocence so I didn't see the demons that stalked my parents like shadows.
I was blinded by the smiles and the masks on the snakes.
I was blinded by love.
I was blinded by trust.
I was blinded by all the MLK movies the public school system fed me in the late 1990's to keep me from knowing about all the other heroes that advocated for me.
I was blinded by the list of the 20 SELECTED negros for me to choose from and do a project on for February.
As if they were the only ones who mattered.
I was blinded by the big light on the cop car as a voice yelled "go in the house!"
Not because I committed a crime, but because the voice thought I might commit one.
I was blinded as the left hand threw dirt in my eyes, so the right hand could dig in my pocket.
I was blinded by one side of the story so I couldn't see the other two.

I was blinded by breasts, so I didn't see her lack of heart.
I was blinded by booty, so I didn't see her lack of backbone.
I was blinded by the story Fox News painted, so I didn't get to see what lay on the other canvases.
I was blind.
Until I learned I had one more eye that my prescription glasses didn't cover.

To Be Black In Amerikkka

To be black in America.
Is life's greatest challenge.
Like being dry in an ocean.
Or a unicorn at the race tracks.
To be an ace in a deck of red diamonds.
They say you're wild but will always call a spade a
spade.
To be a Rollo in a world full of Stewie Griffins and
Maggie Simpsons.
Good enough to laugh at.
But too black to learn from.
Strong enough to lead your sports teams.
But not strong enough to lead your neighborhood.
Now watch this.
I'm black enough to occupy every slot on the VH1
station with my stereotype antics.
But I'm not white enough for your coveted awards.
And you wonder why we make songs like "they gon
think I won a grammy".
I'm not an angry black man.
Maybe I should be.
It just took me 20 years to see the world for the
first time.
I realized just how many legs I had to stand on
once I got down from the noose society has been
choking us with.

We were BROUGHT here!
Taught to be ugly then mocked for the teachings
we were taught by the ones who taught it!
You love my daughter!
But you hate her father.
Because your wife think he's hotter.
And no matter how much tan you put on white it'll
never be onyx.
I am not Yeshua.
I am but the descendent of a king you kidnapped.
Head bag removed and restraints broken.
You don't hate me.
I'm just a constant reminder of why you hate you.

<u>Judge</u>

I can't decide what's worse.
The fear of being shot in the chest by a man in black that calls me brother.
Or the fear being shot in the back by a man in black who took an oath to protect me.
In school we played a game called would you rather.
Would you rather be harassed by the police because you LOOK like you MIGHT be a criminal?
Or would you rather be harassed by a group of men because you LOOK like you MIGHT have a few dollars on you?
No officer I don't sell drugs.
No Ms. Dennis I don't sell drugs.
No I'm not high I just like to laugh.
No I'm not high I just like to eat.

I just can't decide what's worse.
Being friendzoned because I LOOK like "I got hoes", so I might hurt her feelings.
Or being rejected because the last man cheated on her so now all men are trash.
Let's play another game of would you rather.
Would You rather be judged by the actions of my last woman, because I got a feeling you MIGHT hurt me too?
Or would you rather I cheat behind your back and dog you out before you get a chance to do it to me so I can say I did it first?

No baby, i'm not sleeping with that girl who liked my status.
No lil hoe I don't wanna talk to you.
No I'm not flirting with her I'm just being a gentleman.
No I'm not tryna sleep with you I just gave you a compliment.

I cannot Decide What's worse.
Being too black to debate about politics with the suburbanites because I come from public school.
Or being too black to pick books over sports.
One last game of would you rather.

Would you rather be followed in Macy's by the store manager just because you're wearing a black sweatsuit?
Or would you rather I say "screw all white people because they don't like us!"?
No! I did not drop out of school
No! I do not play basketball and football
No! I'm not a criminal just because my hood is black
No! I'm not a racist just because your known to be one.
The fact of the matter is you don't know me, unless I show you who I am!
So judge ME, the way that YOU want to be judged!

Jury

Every body wanna scream "fuck 12 fuck 12"
Until a group of 12 decides on your freedom.

We all scream "fuck 12 fuck 12"
Until 12 hands carry our casket to that hole in the ground.

Minutes it only took you 1, to
Load up that pump action shotgun and push 8 shells out on 4 men.
Did Blizz yell fuck 12 when he was waving that 12 gage?
I got one question.
Who made y'all pure?
Why do a dozen strangers get to play god with my life?
Who made you good enough to pass judgement on me?
I know I said one but I thought I'd add two more.
See everybody wants to play jury duty.
You want to make a rational decision on what kind of a man I am, but you don't know me!
You a judge without a law degree!
Nothing but a volunteer decision maker!
With no real qualifications as to why your opinion matters!
What does juror number 6 know about the sacrifices I've made in vain for my family?

Does juror number 2 know about the good work I
do in my community?
You don't know me!
Only whatever image the opposition has painted of
me.
Another opinion.
Who am I?
What are my goals?
My hobbies?
My responsibilities?
My unfinished work?
You don't got the answer sway!

Fuck 12 strangers who are just as flawed as me,
that have made mistakes before, but feel justified
in deciding my fate!
Fuck who's hands carry me in the epilogue if you
didn't help me fight to survive in the previous
chapters!
If only god can judge me.......
Who are you to be my jury?

<u>History</u>

Too many taxes in the main land.
Wondering what else is out there.
This side was sent to find out what's there.
This side was sent as an exile.
All parties involved were drunk with opportunity.
Bullied by local law men.
Found occupation in anticipation of vacancy.
Bullied in the name of your bully.
Discriminated in the name of the discriminator.
Out with the old.
In with the new.
Finally caught by the problem that gave chase.
The irony.
To run and then chase.
To be robbed and then steal.
In search of freedom, only found slaves.
Gave it a pretty name.
"Liberation"
Human beings turned property.
Property turned cattle.
Tax men came to collect.
From Orange to tangerine.
Same thing just smaller.
Thirteen colonies said "enough is enough!"
"Give me liberty or give me death!"
Free men "liberated" from Jamaica.
To their cries you were deaf!
They got only death!
Broken promises and unfilled amendments!

Laws prepared for men, but men we were not!
At least in your eyes.
Continued to rape mommy!
Continued to attack daddy!
Light skinned spawns you thought nothing of!
Who's the original deadbeat?
Forefathers killed more fathers.
Your fathers, poor fathers.
All this you say is white Christ will.
Civil War was slave war.
Took the crabs out the bucket.
Kept the band's on the claws though.
Fast forward.
We are not equal.
You, judge a tiger on his underwater skills.
You, poured oil on my flower.
Called it stupid for not blooming.
We, once considered strange fruit, made
pomegranate lemonade out of your bitter asses.
Took your daughters and trained them to serve us
as masters.
Selma was one big chess game.
News crew lights broadcasted the oppression
Hashtag Let me vote Bitch!
Offsprings, Princes and princesses continued on
with the kings mission.
Followers of Detroit Red said "We is us and us is
we."
"We protect us and us will feed we."
Hoover was nothing but a high ranking crooked
cop!

The Republicans fucked us hard!
The Democrats made love to us!
Either way we screwed.
My black life only mattered to you behind a dollar.
You still Couldn't stop us from telling our ghetto stories.
In the words of my forefathers.
"Fight the powers that be!"
"Fuck the police!"
"'Thug life!"
"We buy a way out of jail but can't buy freedom."
Last but not least
"Fuck Donald Trump, yea nigga fuck Donald Trump"
The only difference between black history, and American history,
Is the narrator.

<u>Makeup Rag</u>

She left all her insecurities on that makeup rag.
Wiped it all off her face.
The 6 shots of Hennesey from her forehead.
The 3 mixed drinks from her cheekbones that
drowned in that powder and bronzer.
All the self consciousness in her eye liner.
All the self confidence in her lipstick.

Five hours prior she prepared her mask.
Laid the foundation first then added some things I
can't name because...... I don't know everything
about makeup.
I figured the paint is used to make up an image
somewhat different than what she first saw in the
mirror.
Why hide the foundation god blessed you with?
Maybe she doesn't hide it.
I think the cream is called concealer though.
Melanin don't come in a bottle and if he can't see
your natural glow he doesn't deserve to bask in
your presence.
I don't mean to disrespect anybody who likes MAC
products.
I just like to appreciate art.
So of course Imma trip when I see someone put lip
gloss on the Mona Lisa.
All because a blind man didn't like the way it
looked on her.
I want you to love you for who you are.

I want you to seek a man that will love you for who
you are, but first you gotta be comfortable showing
it to him.
I have every right to get offended.
When you approach me with hair you weren't born
with.
Over the counter eyelashes and contacts.
With a body trainer under your tights.
And a face it took you an hour to make.
Just to insult me by saying "I'm not a real man."
How dare you!
I ain't mad at you sister.
I'm mad at the people around you.
Because they want you to be this image, and me?
I wanna know the girl in the mirror.
After she wipes that smirk off her face.

<u>As You Are</u>

She came to me.
She came to me in a dimly lit room under the most
unassuming pretenses.
She said "hi my name is..." I said "I know.."
I said "Hi, I'm....."she said, "I know."
From that moment I was smitten.
Her beauty, encased in the finest Crystal, too pure
to be smudged by mortal hands but too pure to not
be glorified by all those who were blessed enough
to have a glimpse.
In this dimly lit room full of 74 people I saw only
her.
And although I didn't know at the time...she saw
me.

I adored her.
Not the physical but everything she was and is.
I deemed myself unworthy.
I deemed myself not righteous enough to share her
oxygen, for she was of the fairest and I mere
garbage.
I, clapped and applauded her.
I, praised and worshipped her.
I knew there was more and more and more to her.
I...saw her bleeding.
I yearned to be that cloth with which she covered
her cuts.
I would have rather taken those cuts for her.
I wanted to be for her.

I saw a star fall out of the sky and I wished upon it
as it declined that I would be fortunate enough to
cross paths with the goddess.
I watched in agony!
As my affection crawled through the abyss and
despair.
Mud! on her Crystal casing!
Slime! Across the bottom of it!
Leeches! Snails! Bottom feeders!
Working to slip through the cracks and
contaminate my beloved!

I in the meantime trained.
Trained my mind and spirit for whatever was to
come, because even though I didn't know how or
why I knew I was on a path.
While walking I searched for her.
I searched and searched until finally I discovered
her.
I was disturbed to see that the abyss had damaged
the beauty of which I lust.
But though fractured, thine spirits were not
completely severed.

She came to me.
She came to me bruised and drained under the
most vulnerable pretenses.
I said..."I miss you." she said "I know."
She said "I miss you..." I said "I know."
Though she was THERE she wasn't HERE.
She wasn't yet restored to her glory and I......ached.

I ached knowing her to soar so high above the ground, but to see her fluttering with those unworthy.

I found myself entering the abyss.
I couldn't go forward but I couldn't turn away and while walking, the wolf discarded the sheep skin it wore and showed teeth.
Ice cold blue veins and silver fangs, with my bleeding heart dripping onto her fur and into the snow.
I slowly.....stalked.....away...
Into the familiar abyss.
Kicking myself for seeing a sheep and loving a wolf.
But refusing to question why the sheep only ate meat!
And always peeked at the grass on the other lawns while ignoring what she stood on.
I sank into the abyss and that's when.

She came to me.
She came to me under the most humble and compassionate pretenses.
I said"....your bleeding..." she said "I know."
She said "your bleeding" I said "I know".
She confessed to me all that I felt for her and then....we began.
After years of admiring each other from afar we began healing each other.

After years of yearning it was I who held the cloth
in place to cover her scars!
It was she, who picked me up when I was down!
It was I, who uplifted her once standing!
It was her, who reached to the heavens, and
handed me a piece of sunshine!
It was I, that removed the Excalibur from her
chest, after many had tried and many had failed.
It was her, that made me keep believing in myself.

She came to me.
She came to me under the most empathetic
pretenses.
She said "..I love you."
I said "..I love you too."
And one night...we professed it.
Her and I locked in a trance where seconds were
minutes and minutes were hours.
Our bodies and chi intricately woven and
intertwined together.
The connection was confirmed!
What I knew that she wouldn't see is that I wanted
her not CONSIDERING her scars but..BECAUSE of
her scars!
She laid out her faults.
I said "I want you as you are."
She laid out her weakness.
I said "I want you as you are."
She showed me her vulnerabilities.
"I want you as you are."
She showed me the inside of her casing.

"I want you as you are."
Because she never once questioned the condition
of me!
She never thought I not good enough!
She never thought I not worthy!
She never thought I too insignificant for her!
It was her..who felt not good enough!

Show me your broken heart and all your scars Baby
I'll take you as you are.
Show me your broken heart and all your scars
Baby I'll take you as you are.

Pretty Bird

The city heard.
Soft cries from a pretty bird.
From Peoples street to 23rd.
She tweets because she's free and she cries,
because she's caged.
Caged in a zone of discomfort and rage.
And every day the bypassers mock the sweet bird.
And everyday she cries out her cry, the canary
sings of survival.
And crooned of a time before her incarceration.
She once lived free, soaring through the
macaronesian islands,
And if she closed her eyes she could still smell the
salt water of the Atlantic coast.
A majestic time it was...

But when she opens her eyes she sees only the hell
that the people around her call a zoo.
Which in her opinion is no more than a glorified
prison!
So she puts on a smile....
And a dance....
And a tune...
And all the while they clap...
And applaud...
She suffers.....
And every night she cries her song of survival.
She fantasizes of the cage door swinging open so
that she can flee!

Declare the skies that she once soared once more,
and take in the unpolluted air.
Oh, how the pretty bird is a dreamer.
One night came a prophet.
He sought not jewels or money, only liberty.
In the still of the night he ventured deep into the
zoo.
When no one was around to hear the pretty bird
cry.
When he opened the cage, the bird ceased to sing.
And he only had this to say.

Fly away pretty bird!
Tweet loud when you cry!
Fly away pretty bird!
Live free in the sky!
Fly away pretty bird!
Pretty song in the night!
Fly away pretty bird!
Pretty please don't die!

<u>Killing Me Softly</u>

Detailing my pain with her pencil.
Scripting my life with her notebook.
Killing me softly with her poem.
Killing me softly, with her poem.
Telling my whole life.....

With her metaphors and smilies.
Simply carving a curvy line across my membrane.
Like chalk on a board as she scribbles in her
notebook.
She's a murderer!
I was invited to watch the public execution, only to
realise that it was I to be placed in the guillotine.
Dark shades, covered her face as the executioner
dealt out the sentence, she.
Killed me softly with her poem.
Neck nestled in the contraption, I gazed into the
audience and felt the world shrinking.
The air around me thinning, as everyone is
spinning
And the more poetry she releases into the
atmosphere, the more effective the spores of her
metaphors.
It was as if she was reading my tweets from 2:49
am.
I stared, teary eyes pleading that she stopped but
my heart galloped when she continued. She, killed
me softly with her poem and I enjoyed the pain.

A masochist I became as the poet described all of my agony!
She, carved my scars!
She, cried my tears!
She, understood!
The pain of a thousand broken promises slicing against the flesh.
And the sigh, the sigh of relief you release before the next lash catches you off guard.
She understood!
Which in a world full of suffering was all I ever wanted.
And with my last breath,
Eyes muddied with tears and stick like eyelashes clinging to the dampness.
Through blurry eyes I whispered, "thank you".
As the slice of the guillotine razor brought the show to an end.

D.O.P.E

I cooked this up in the same pot that I had to piss in.

My mama's special spoon was the only silver in the kitchen.

The same belt she shot up with is the same one that whipped us.

The black lips from the glass pipe are the ones who tried to kiss us.

I'm The bastard child of an alcoholic junkie.

From the due date mom and dad didn't want me.

He had more seeds to sow, he was only thinking about plan b.

When I was 3 my mama gave me to another family.

I'm that last few shakes of powder In the dime bag.

That, black stain on the big spoon from where the fire was at.

The residue left on the sides of the coffee pot.

That, nasal drip that never go away whether its cold or not.

Coming straight out of section 8! Another crack baby on medication!

Who survived public housing and public education!

Conceived by it, grew up, and the he sold,

And by this last white line his name you should know it's....

Part Two: #MBTM

<u>The Man Behind The Mask</u>

Now this man is a bit.....different than your usual poet. The Man Behind The Mask, or MBTM for short, is a tortured soul to say the least. One of the world's forgotten children this man has suffered and survived not only the struggles of poverty, but also the throes of depression and several other psychological diagnosis'. After years of solitary he went and searched for others like himself. Other children forgotten and abandoned by the world.

Casted out by society, and disdained by blood relatives. Eventually he found his tribe. Tho scattered they still existed. He decided to shoulder the burden of their message. To be a pioneer for the outsiders. In order for the revolution to succeed, he first needed to open the world's eyes,

<u>Who Can I Cry To</u>

Tell me who can I cry to, when I don't know who to trust.

Tell me who can I cry to, when I don't know who to love.

Tell me who can I cry to, that will have the right words today.

Tell me who can I cry to, right here right now today.

Tell me who can I cry to, when I feel alone and weak.

Tell me who can I cry to, when I don't have the voice to speak.

Tell me who can I cry to, when I don't know what to do.

Tell me who can I cry to, tell me can I cry to you.

<u>Depression Sometimes</u>

Depression isnt always suicidal thoughts.
Sometimes it's a vibe.
Sometimes it's staying in the house all day.
Sometimes it's never leaving the bed for days at a
time.
Sometimes it's not eating all day
Sometimes it's not returning calls or texts of loved
ones.
Sometimes it's not showering, not smiling, not
thinking, not wanting, not feeling,
not...........anything.

Depression isnt always suicidal thoughts.
Sometimes it's memes.
Sometimes its gifs and subliminal posts, and
shares, and comments.
Or lack thereof.
Sometimes..... depression is poems like this......

Pills

I was fine before they put me on pills at nine.
Now I'm 25 with..
Major depression,
Abandonment issues,
Anxiety,
Paranoia,
IED maybe,
Skitzo maybe,
ADHD Maybe,
Bi polar maybe,
Try more of,
Your poison.
You prescribed the remedy
but neglected to reveal the antidote,
From one pill to three to four pills in a cup,
While my family tells me "he WILL toughen up",
School counselor telling us, these pills ain't
enough.
I watched my father drive past me everyday In a
clean cadillac while I couldn't get bullies off my
ass!
Maybe that kid deserves to be sad!
When his mama getting high, and leaves for
months at a time.
And grandma can't tell you why!
Everyone is leaving, why!?
What's wrong with me?
I was nine, I was supposed to cry!

Grandpop was the only one who wanted me and he died!
I was supposed to cry!
My best friend was my dog and he died!
I was supposed to cry!
How am I supposed to "man up"?
I'm just a kid!
With no father, no brothers, and no real friends.
What do you mean don't cry when you whipping my ass?
What do you mean don't cry when I'm feeling sad?
What do you mean don't cry when I'm bleeding?
This shit hurts!
I'm supposed to cry!
I was fourteen he was twenty eight, his fist cracked the bones in my face!
I was supposed to cry!
I got beatings at school because I wasn't tough.
And then beatings at home because I cried at school.
Maybe there's nothing wrong with me.
Maybe there's something wrong with you.
I was fine before they put me on pills at nine.
Now I'm 25......with a message.

Deafth

Nobody hears those silent cries for help.
Those, quiet scribbles and scrapes in that
notebook.
Those, small keyboard vibrations as you type that
subliminal online post that nobody is going to like
or comment on.
Nobody hears.
That scream of agony muffled by the mask you
wear to keep people from seeing the flaws.
No I'm not fine! I'm not ok!
It's just easier to tell you I am rather than explain
my anxiety.
And it's not like you'll understand anyway.
Nobody hears!
I'm living and talk to the dead but still No one
hears.
The whispers screaming "do it!"
The screams whispering "he's too scared to do it."
All you hear is me......
Choking on the word help.

<u>These Scars</u>

So I asked my beloved....."You wanna know how I got these scars?"

I was a scared little boy in a scary little place.

With scabs on my hands and blood on my face.

Until one day...everything changed.

In school I was suspended ten days at a time and while home for two weeks mother let me do NOTHING!

I had no friends!

No one to talk to!

Just me my thoughts....... and a razor.

The other kids they hated me...

My sisters they hated me...and.

In time I believed it and I....hated.....me!!

I decided I wasn't a good boy, and bad boys needed to be punished.

So I took the razor and asked myself..... "Do you deserve to live?...... Or do you deserve to die?"

My beloved looked shocked.

Mouth open, heart thumping, beads of sweat racing each other down her temple.

She asks, "what happens next?".....

You know My mother was no scholar but she was born no fool either.

You see she would always tell me how I had this habit of bottling everything up and Up and UP!

Until it all EXPLODED from the pressure!

And she was right!

I lashed out at any and all who were close enough
to hear me roar!
I loved it!!
I THRIVED on it!!
But these outbursts....... came with consequences.
And consequences........ came with punishment.
And punishment....... came with bad thoughts.
And i told myself "these thoughts this razor and
me...are going to have a party."
You see mother always said that I was too smart
for my own good, and indeed I was because,
I found a shortcut.
I found a way to relieve the pressure silently.
To SPILL the extras in smaller amounts.
Not with words but with BLOOD!!
Beautiful bright blood trickling across me like
condensation on a crystal glass.....
Oh don't look at me like that......It gets better.
One day I do it....because I deserved it.
The next day I do it......because I still thought bad
thoughts..
But the day after that.......I didn't do it because I
deserved it
No no no NO! I did it because I wanted it!!
I wanted the sting!
The smell of the sanitized metal.
Just thinking about it now makes me hard and
excited!
The pleasant sting.
From the razor's edge when the blood splashed.
And no that's not a wrestling scheme.

I wanted, that feeling...
That... air leaving the bag slowly.......hissing away...
Slowly.... dragging the blade....
Slowly.....fading away.
Because I'm a worthless piece of shit.
And I should be grateful that I'm alive.
I'm nothing....
And I'm blessed....
Because I could be dead...
Which means these feelings wouldn't exist.
Which means..... one day it'll get better.
But until that day....
I have eighteen ounces of blood at my disposal.
That I will dispatch one lone streak at a time.

Take It Off

Take it off!
The words sent chills through her spine.
As she remembered every night he came in and
announced those three words.

Take it off!
He was supposed to protect her, love her, save her.
Instead he threatened her, molested her, raped
her.
Silently sent dirty looks at the dinner table when
mom wasn't looking.
The slimy remarks in the summer as she walks
past the couch in her shorts.
She refuses to keep up her hygiene in the hopes
that it will thwart him off.
Mom said a lady shouldn't smell this way.
Get in the bathroom and shower!

Take it off!
Now that she's older she wears her attitude tightly
on her face.
She doesn't want to be bothered.
Her boyfriend wants second and third base, but
flashbacks of being touched in the dugout has her
nervous at bat.
She loves him....
But she won't trust him because the last man that
was supposed to protect her........didn't.
He can see the mask.... So he tells her.

42

Take it off!
Please for me!
But never again will she be victim to a man.

Take it off!
The words echoed over the bass.
She steps over dollar bills and tries her best to
focus on the lights and not the vultures reaching
out to her.
Work doesn't come easy when studying for a
degree.
So she does what she has to to beat starvation.
It's not her fault.
The world made her this way.
She hates herself for being this way.
Now every night the music plays, and the money
rains, she hears those three haunting words...

Take it off!
When she gets home to a safe place she tries to
take off the mask but,
It's hard to tell where the mask ends and her face
begins.
So she looks in the mirror...
And tells her reflection...
Take it off!

<u>Weekday Skit</u>

I tried to cut myself on Monday.
But I picked up the knife with the dull blade.
I tried to hang myself on Tuesday.
But the belt snapped when I kicked the stool away.
On Wednesday I put a gun in my hand.
But on Thursday the muthafucking glock jammed.
Friday I took a hand full of vicodin.
And on Sunday imma try the knife again.

I face timed my daughter on Sunday.
We blew kisses through the phone on Sunday.
Went to see Pop grave on Monday.
I know that we gon meet again one day.
Now I'm drinking by myself in the darkness.
Since my baby cheated on me I been heartless.
And this liquor got a n***a feeling thoughtless.
Russian Roulette with 2 in the revolver.

I tried to cut myself on Monday.
But I picked up the knife with the dull blade.
I tried to hang myself on Tuesday.
But the belt snapped when I kicked the stool away.
On Wednesday I put a gun in my hand.
But on Thursday the muthafuckin glock jammed.
Friday I took a hand full of vicodin.
And on Sunday imma try the knife again.

My grandma told me put my faith in Jesus.
The Lord is always here he'll never leave us.

When I was fourteen years I got my skull cracked.
Tell me grandmom where the fuck was God at?
I was eleven in the mental ward screaming.
The nurses all said I was demon.
I only heard the voices in my head.
Tell me grandma where the hell was God at?

I tried to cut myself on Monday.
But I picked up the knife with the dull blade.
I tried to hang myself on Tuesday.
But the belt snapped when I kicked the stool away.
On Wednesday I put a gun in my hand.
But on Thursday the muthafuckin glock jammed.
Friday I took a hand full of vicodin.
And on Sunday imma try the knife again.

<u>**Anxiety**</u>

You won't relate to this.
If you do than we're brothers and sisters in arms
in this war.
I can't........relax.
My hands are shaking, I'm...... stuttering, sweating,
twitching pacing, heartbeat racing.
While everyone is staring and asking "what's
wrong?"
My Tongue is tied in a knot and my mouth is dry
so
I can't fix this
And they're getting more impatient waiting and
waiting.
Until finally, I utter the wrong words.
Stupid!
Dammit I'm thirsty!

You won't relate to this.
I'm exhausted for no reason, yet I'm full of energy.
I begged and pleaded not to be sent to the place
where they strap you to the bed.
Just to stay home and refuse to get out of bed.
The restraints here are mental.
I have the energy to run and do..........things.
But I can't get out of this freaking bed!
Sheet turned mud!
Blanket to seaweed!
It binds me!

These thoughts are Chinese finger traps and
quicksand.
The more I panic the worse it gets!
Don't you get it?
Why don't you get it?
Forget it!
I'll just sit here and rock and shake for a few hours.
Until I finally calm down enough to lay still.

Don't worry you won't relate to this.
I'm alone and being followed at the same time.
I'm half asleep and charged up at the same time.
Out of breath and out of motivation at the same
time.
Too tired to get up, too hyper to relax.
I need to pee, but I need to stay here.
I need some water, but I need to stay here.
I need help, but I need to stay here.
And everytime my phone vibrates and it asks
"wyd" I say....
"I'm chilling."

<u>Smile</u>

Smile baby.
Missing my daughter while holding her doll baby
with my other hand holding a razor.
I'm not committing suicide.
Sometimes you just gotta stare those demons in
the face while holding on to your motivation.
Never mind that temptation.
I know you anxious.
And the devil and hell is waiting.
All it takes is.....
One swipe, for one life, than you're on your way!
But.....
The baby is waiting too.....
YOUR BABY is waiting for YOU.

Smile baby.
Reminiscing on my alcoholic mother's advice while
I drink straight from the bottle.
My my my how the circle closes.
I'm not an alcoholic.
I just refuse to smoke because it took so many of
my loved ones.
I just refuse to do drugs because it took away so
many of my loved ones.
Some to the grave and some to the cage.
So I choose the lesser of three evils to wash my
sins away.
Fighting to focus because it's time to perform.

The people are waiting.
YOUR FANS are waiting for YOU.

So Just smile baby.
Because they'll never know your shoulders have
exceeded the weight limit.
They'll never notice your big toe peeking over the
ledge as you wait for the wind to push harder.
They'll always applaud you for being so strong and
never having anything wrong but,
They'll always never stop and ask how are you
REALLY DOING.
All they'll see.......is this smile.

Beautiful Scars

Standing alone on a crowded Boulevard.
Thousands of people walking up and down left and
right.
Blood, cascades down my right and left forearms.
Beautiful scars on critical veins.

First go around, mom interrupted.
They carted me away to the nut house for my
second visit.
Mother!
I found joy in the pain!
It let me know that this wasn't a dream, and that I
really do feel this unbelievable amount of pain.
Punishment, I felt as though I deserved for all that
I loved was lunch for the maggots.
Antisocial psychopath. I ate lunch with the nerds
and fat kids.
Kids who hated me, made me hate myself for being
hated!
Crimson stains on the razor blade of my pencil
sharpener kept the animal fed.
Beautiful scars on critical veins.

Torturing myself to see how well I can take the
pain.
Every time hurts a little less than the last time.
Scratches and scars hide, on arms and on thighs.
Bet mom won't see these.
Dope rhymes on cds kept me breathing in hard

times.

Locked in my room listening to 50 Cent tell me how it goes down in his hood.

Batman fan, though I grew up to be more like the Joker and Zsasz.

Like mother, I had an affliction for the steel.

Mine was a blade!

Her's was a spoon in her drawer she THOUGHT she hid well.

Both of us stayed locked in our rooms for days at a time.

Now I see how we never saw each other on the other side of that same coin.

While she got high.... I got low.

If only I knew my mother sat on that same see-saw with me.

Beautiful scars on critical veins.

That cold steel, tempts me like a shapely woman on the weekend.

Begging me to go ahead and take a STAB AT IT!

Slice vertically this time, instead of horizontal.

Some lines I can't help but cross.

Tattooing my hobby with no ink or gun.

Just blades, that I've sharpened on the concrete.

Wiped thoroughly with the same alcohol pads I used to clean my games and cds.

Who needs drugs, when I have you?

Blissful stinging and burning to remind me that the hell I live in isn't that bad.

Rather than end my story,

The Man The Mask The Myth

I will broadcast it for the world to see,
And maybe they'll learn from me,
The stories behind these homemade tattoos which
reads,
Beautiful scars on Critical veins

Epilogue: Snack Zaddy

#<u>SnackZaddy</u>

OK this guy, not the one you want to leave your girlfriend around. Slick Talker, intelligent, humorous, we could go on and on with this guy. Once a shy little caterpillar with mild mannered thoughts in his mind about the girls in his class. He has now metamorphosed into a confident young butterfly, with enough swagger to sweet talk the panties off of mother Teresa! He has manifested a reputation amongst the ladies as a suave gentleman. Romantic, polite, a mother's dream and a daughter's fantasy.

However, do not mistake the wolf for a sheep, because he too has a darkside. One that is polluted with Bondage, Dominance, and much much more. We will save him for the next book, but for now enjoy this sneak preview.

Potion No.20

I want to kiss your soul.
Let me peel back the layers of your troubles and
lick your worries away.
Spill your concerns onto my lips and let it run
down my beard and neck.
Release your sorrow, and exhale your pain, while I
autograph my name onto your love with my
tongue.
As I roll my affection back and forth left and right I
want you to vent to me.
Tell me how it feels...
Tell me where to turn....
Direct me to your soul...
Let me glide my tongue down your spirit and up
your nature until the sun has breakfast.
You see I know your pretty.
And your body is amazing!
But I think your soul is beautiful.
The poetry you recite and,
The melodies from your windpipes make me want
to suck on your imagination and lick the
afterthoughts off the sides as they trickle down.
I want to kiss your soul.
The sweet smell of your creative process.
You called it potion #20.
It's not your body I want, it's what's on the inside.

Beauty is only skin deep but beyond that, is heavens door.

Let me fill my grail at your fountain of youth, as I lap at your oasis.

Oh what I would give to pitch a tent at your pond.

I would drown!

A happy man!

With your knees against my ears and your hips in my hands as I squeeze harder BEGGING you for more.

.....There's a place between sober and high that the potion takes me.

You know that soft place where you feel at ease but still aware of the surroundings.

I want to kiss your soul.

I've been very stressed lately and what I need right now is a dose of your potion.

No Tylenol, advil, or Sudafed.

Not at all, just my skills ,and you in the bed.

Reveal to me Pandora's box, so I may slurp the treasures from the velvet walls.

I have a particular thirst I need quenching.

Reach up to the shelf and grab potion number 20 for me.

Because when I come.....

You'll cum.....

And when I'm done.....

Your numb.....

When I kiss your soul.....

I taste....

Potion #20

To Be Continued........

Made in the USA
Middletown, DE
30 December 2023

46154922R00035